F'UN EXAMS

F'UN EXAMS

The Best Funny Exam Answers from Scotland

IAN BLACK

BLACK & WHITE PUBLISHING

First published 2012
by Black & White Publishing Ltd
29 Ocean Drive, Edinburgh EH6 6JL

3 5 7 9 10 8 6 4 2   16 17 18 19

Reprinted 2016

ISBN   978 1 84502 489 5

A CIP catalogue record for this book is available
from the British Library.

Typeset by RefineCatch Limited, Bungay
Printed and bound by CPI Group (UK) Ltd, Croydon, CR0 4YY

CONTENTS

ARTS

Q Describe a work of John Constable.

A The Haywain is a right good Constable painting. It is a comment on the state of the roads in the eighteenth century. The horse and cartie are stuck in the middle of a humungous dub.

In an essay on Polish theatre director Jerzy Grotowski and his 'laboratory theatre' which required a physically demanding style of acting, one student wrote about actor Ryszard Cieslak:

'straining at his role in the lavatory theatre'.

Q What looks like half an apple?

A *The half that's left.*

A drama class was doing an end-of-year test. One of the questions was a list of names/terms that the pupils had to describe in their own words. One of the words was 'Gobo'.

One of the pupils wrote: '*A character from Lord of the Rings who is a skitzo.*'

What can a vegetarian never eat for breakfast?

 His tea.

 If you throw a blue stone into the Red Sea what will it become?

 Soakin.

Q How can a man go eight days without sleeping?

A He sleeps at night, except if he is on the nightshift. I don't know what he does then. Women can do this too.

Q How can you lift an elephant with one hand?

A Elephants hwny got hands. A trunk, aye, hands naw.

How can you drop a raw egg onto a concrete floor without cracking it?

 It would need to be an awfy big egg to crack a concrete floor. Don't know.

F'UN GREAT ONES

2. A 3-kg object is released from rest at a height of 5m on a curved frictionless ramp. At the foot of the ramp is a spring of force constant k = 100 N/m. The object slides down the ramp and into the spring, compressing it a distance x before coming to rest.

10 (a) Find x.
5 (b) Does the object continue to move after it comes to rest? If yes , how high will it go up the slope before it comes to rest?

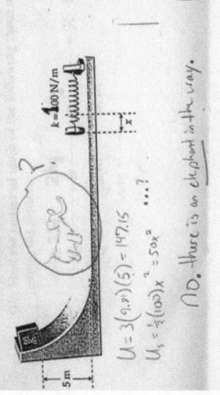

$U = 3(9.81)(5) = 147.15$

$U_s = \frac{1}{2}(100)x^2 = 50x^2 \cdots ?$

NO. there is an elephant in the way.

F'UN GREAT ONES

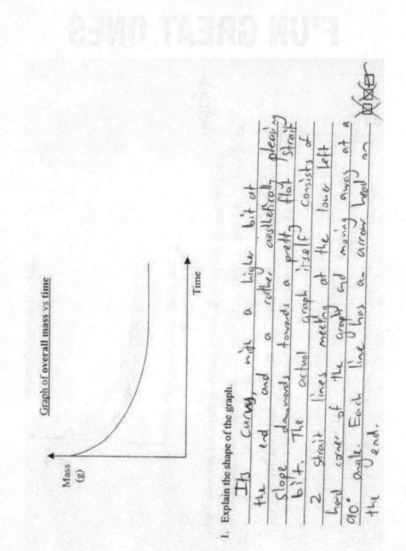

Graph of overall mass vs time

Mass (g)

Time

1. Explain the shape of the graph.

It's curvy, with a higher bit at the end and a rather aesthetically pleasing slope downwards towards a pretty flat straight bit. The actual graph itself consists of 2 strait lines meeting at the lower left hand corner of the graph and going away at a 90° angle. Each line has an arrow head on the dead end.

(ii) Write a balanced half equation for the reaction at the positive electrode.

$$2 + 3 = ?$$

(iii) Write a balanced half equation for the reaction at the negative electrode.

fork + Shoe = Spleen

(iv) Explain why the concentration of sulfate ions increases in the electrolyte?

Aliens. Damn aliens are responsible for everything weird that's going on around here.

Solving equation by

$$\frac{1}{n}\sin x = ?$$

$$\frac{1}{\cancel{n}}\sin\!\!\!\!\!/\, x =$$

$$six = 6$$

F'un Great Ones

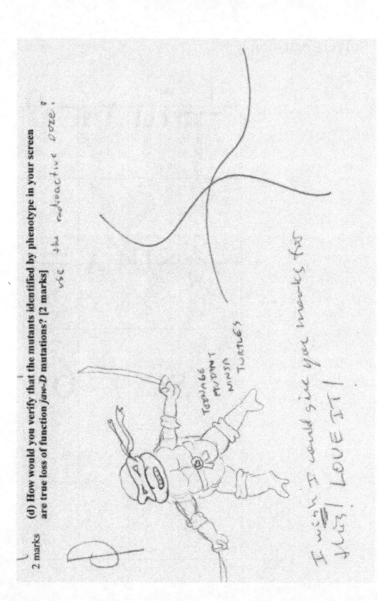

18

What is a vibration?

There are good vibrations and bad vibrations. Good vibrations were discovered in the 1960s

F'un Great Ones

2. Explain ONE of the three ways that clouds can be formed. Used diagrams to help illustrate your answer. (2 marks)

sun

cloud

ground

God

HUMANITIES

Q Give a reason for the population explosion in Scotland in the 1840s.

A There was a population explosion in the 1840s cause they didny huv the telly.

Q Discuss the defensive architecture of Scottish mediaeval castles.

A Because there were no widows in the castles, the archers had to use slits in the walls.

Briefly describe Egypt in the time of the Pharaohs.

 Ancient Egypt was inhabited by mummies and they all wrote in hydraulics. They lived in the Sarah Dessert and travelled by Camelot. The climate of the Sarah meant that the inhabitants had to live somewhere else.

 Describe the position of the settlements in the area.

They are all at the bottom of the Firth of Clyde.

Name a primary cause of WWI.

 The First World War started cause sumbuddy shot the Archduck.

 What is transhumance?

A *Transhumance is when the farmer's cows are taken up to the summer pasture along with the farmer's son and they are left to graze all summer.*

Where was the American Declaration of Independence signed?

 All over the place, like that cheap shop Pennysylvayna, and Washington, but mainly at the bottom.

 Write a short essay on what you would do if you had one hour to live.

If I had one hour to live I'd spend it in this exam because it feels like an eternity.

What is Britain's highest award for valour in war?

 Nelson's Column.

 What is the word for newly born puppies?

 A litre.

Q Why were the Greeks so important in history?

A The Greeks were a highly sculptured people, and without them we wouldn't have history. The Greeks also had myths. A myth is a female moth.

One student suggested that during the Middle Ages '*most books were written on valium*' rather than the more traditional vellum.

[Author's comment: An interesting concept. It was speed in my day.]

Discuss an important Greek.

 Socrates was a famous Greek teacher who went around giving people advice. They killed him. Socrates died from an overdose of wedlock.* After his death, his career suffered a dramatic decline.

[* Teacher's comment: 'I know how he felt.']

 Why were the early days of history called the Dark Ages?

 Because there were so many knights?

Q What did Sir Francis Drake say when told the Spanish were coming?

A *'The Spanish Armada can wait, my bowels can't.'*

A student wrote: '*Spain was a very Catholic country, since Christianity had been taken there in the third century BC*'.

[Author's comment: He or she might know their religious history, but the chronology could use some work!]

Q What happened at Chernobyl?

A *A nuclear rector blew up.*

In a paper on the Cold War a university student wrote: '*In 1945, Stalin began to build a buffet zone around Eastern Europe.*'

[Author's comment: That would take rather a lot of sandwiches and sausage rolls.]

In which sea battle did Admiral Lord Nelson die?

His last one. Duh!

A teacher was explaining literary history in a Scottish school and was telling them about Shakespeare plays and that the females were sometimes played by prostitutes.

A pupil raised her hand and asked: 'What's a prostitute, Miss?'

Teacher fired it straight back and asked the class: 'Who can tell me what a prostitute is?'

Another pupil raised her hand and said: 'Aren't they the opposites of Catholics?'

What does the French phrase *moi aussi* mean?

 I am an Australian.

 Who was Queen Elizabeth?

 Queen Elizabeth was the 'Virgin Queen'. As a queen she was a success. When she exposed herself before her troops they all shouted, 'Hurrah.'

Q Discuss Renaissance writing.

A The greatest writer of the Renaissance was William Shakespeare. He was born in the year 1564, supposedly on his birthday. He wrote trajedies, comedideys, and hysterectomies.

Writing at the same time as Shakespeare was Miguell Cervanti. He wrote Donkey Hote. The next great author was John Milton. Milton wrote Paradise Lost. Then his wife died and he wrote Paradise Regained.

Q What does the word 'benign' mean?

 A Benign is what you will be after you be-eight.

Q Who was Julius Caesar?

A Julius Caesar extinguished himself on the battlefields of Gaul. The Ids of March murdered him because they thought he was going to be made king. Dying, he gasped out: 'Tee hee, Brutus.'

F'un Exams

[From recent French Bac papers. These are all real. *Perles de non-wisdom.*]

Président Mitterand died from cancer of the womb.

Physics was discovered by accident in antiquity by Larry Stottle.

The earth would be covered in ice if it weren't for the volcanoes inside it warming it up.

When a baby is born, it gives a loud cry, like Tarzan in the jungle.

The points of a compass are top, bottom, east and west.

Coca-cola fields run down the water supplies in India.

At the time of the Cold War, it was very cold.

Japan is a big island lost in the middle of the sea.

The surface area of Japan is bigger than France, smaller than New Zealand and about the same as Cuba.

General Aïe Zenhower commanded the disembarkations in 1942 in North Africa. (The French say 'Aïe' for 'ouch'.)

The armistice is a war which ends every year on 11 November.

A septuagenarian is a shape with seven sides.

Socrates was forced to commit suicide himself.

There are two sorts of gas - natural gas and supernatural gas.

In towns, the problem of security is a problem of insecurity.

When there is trouble in the world, the UN sends in the Blue Baseball Hats. (The student wrote 'casquettes bleus' rather than 'casques bleus', which means 'blue berets'.)

Q What are hieroglyphics?

 A I don't know for sure, but they are taller than lowerglyphics.

Q What does the word 'pathos' mean?

A Is he the guy that hings aboot wi Athos an' Aramis?

Define the word 'inspire'.

 When you breathe, you inspire. When you don't breathe, you expire.

Q What is a fossil?

A A fossil is an extinct animal or plant. The older it is, the more extincter it is.

Define momentum.

 A momentum is what you give someone when they are going away.

 What is a co-operative?

 It's a kind of shop that your granny calls 'The Co' and it is not so dear as Marks and Sparks.

Define monotony.

 Monotony means being married to the same wife for all your life. God!

 Use the word 'judicious' in a sentence to show you understand its meaning.

 Hands that judicious can be soft as your face.

Write a sentence using the word 'was' precisely.

 Was is what holds up the roof ae oor hoose.

 Explain what you know about the Hebrews.

 They are islands near the West of Scotland.

A priest in a Glasgow Catholic school was trying to involve the only pupil who had not answered a question. He asked the wee guy (who, unbeknown to his interlocutor, had a speech impediment):

'How many persons are there in the One God?'

The answer comes back: 'The Hagher, the Hun and the Holy Ghost.'

After hearing this for the third time he says to the boy: 'I don't understand, son.'

To which came the reply: 'Yer no hupposed tae. It's a huckin mystery.'

Q Why did the Three Wise Men bring gold to the birth of Jesus?

A To pay for the hotel.

Q What is a Hindu?

A It's the last bird in a homing pigeon race.

Q What language is the Qu'ran written in?

A *Braille. I can't read it, but.*

Q Name a place of pilgrimage that Christians go to.

A *Christians go on pilgrimage to Lord's.*

What was unusual about the reign of
Queen Victoria?

Queen Victoria was the longest queen.
She sat on the thorn for sixty-three
years. She was a moral woman who
practised virtue. Her death was the
final event which ended her reign.

Q Explain the saying: 'The sun never sets on the British Empire.'

A The sun never set on the British Empire because the British Empire is in the East and the sun sets in the West.

Q Who was Charles Darwin?

A Charles Darwin was a naturist who wrote the Organ of the Species.

F'UN GREAT ONES

20. Women should periodically have a Pap smear test performed to detect cervical cancer. Which letter indicates the cervix in the diagram below?

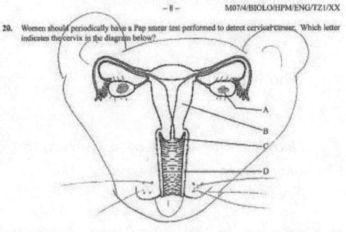

21. In human embryo development, what is the approximate time span between fertilization and implantation of the blastocyst?

A. 12 days

B. 7 days

C. 72 hours

D. 36 hours

Hard and Soft Water

1. Briefly explain what hard water is. *ice*

_____

_____

_____

_____

(ii) In which of these two steps does reduction of titanium occur? _____2_____

Explain your answer. *The calcuble probability of*
getting this answer correct was 50%.
good enough.

(d) Explain why phosphorus trichloride (PCl₃) is polar.

God made it that way.

_____

_____

_____

(b) *Sea salt is commercially obtained from sea water by the process of evaporation and crystallization. The main component of sea salt is sodium chloride.*

What type of attractive force or bond holds the sodium ions and chloride ions together in a crystal of sodium chloride?

James bond.

4. The solid figure below can best be described as: _pac-man_

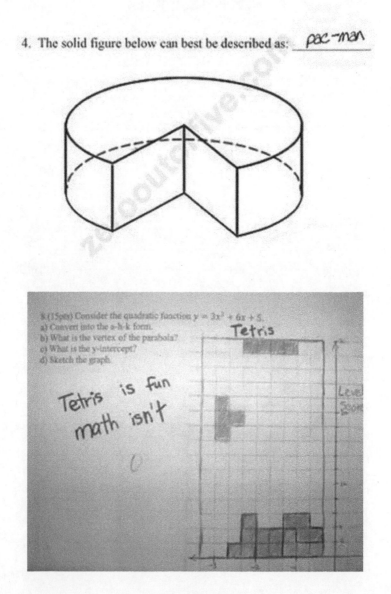

8. (15pts) Consider the quadratic function $y = 3x^2 + 6x + 5$.
a) Convert into the a-h-k form.
b) What is the vertex of the parabola?
c) What is the y-intercept?
d) Sketch the graph.

Tetris

Tetris is fun
math isn't

Level
Score

1 To find a woman you need Time and Money therefore:

$$\text{Woman} = \text{Time} \times \text{Money}$$

2 "Time is money" so

$$\text{Time} = \text{Money}$$

3 Therefore

$$\text{Woman} = \text{Money} \times \text{Money}$$

$$\text{Woman} = (\text{Money})^2$$

4 "Money is the root of all problems"

$$\text{Money} = \sqrt{\text{Problems}}$$

5 Therefore

$$\text{Woman} = \left(\sqrt{\text{Problems}}\right)^2$$

$$\text{Woman} = \text{Problems}$$

(A⁺)

A proton approaches a long line of positive charge so that with it's initial trajectory it would intersect the line. The line has a uniform charge density of 5 nanoC/m. If the proton starts off with velocity 300 km/s a distance 1 km from the line charge, what is the distance of closest approach?

Mass of proton=1.67E-27 kg

K=8.99E9 Nmm/CC

Hint: find the field and potential that affect the proton.

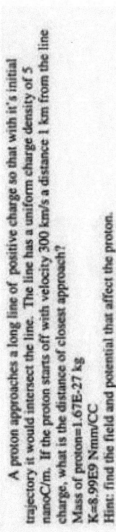

Problem

Use calculus to find the identity of Batman.

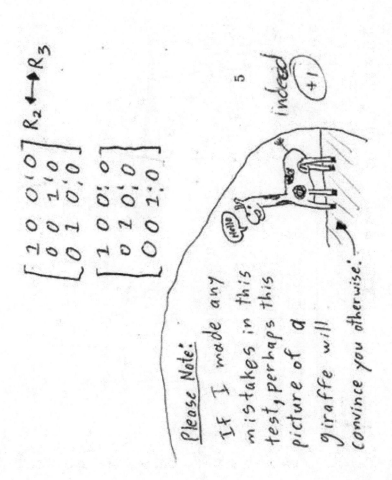

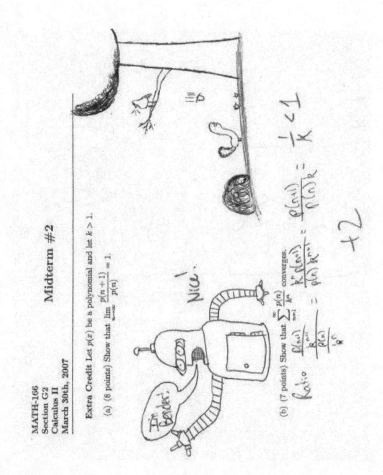

MATH-166
Section G2
Calculus II
March 30th, 2007

Midterm #2

Extra Credit Let $p(x)$ be a polynomial and let $k > 1$.

(a) (8 points) Show that $\lim\limits_{n \to \infty} \dfrac{p(n+1)}{p(n)} = 1$.

Nice!

(b) (7 points) Show that $\sum\limits_{n=1}^{\infty} \dfrac{p(n)}{k^n}$ converges.

Ratio: $\dfrac{\frac{p(n+1)}{k^{n+1}}}{\frac{p(n)}{k^n}} = \dfrac{k^n \, p(n+1)}{p(n) \, k^{n+1}} = \dfrac{p(n+1)}{p(n) \cdot k} = \dfrac{1}{k} < 1$

Dr. Gender,

+2

52

MATHEMATICS

In the current financial climate, what guarantees may The Royal Bank of Scotland insist on as security?

 If you are buying a house they will insist that you are well endowed.

 Name four activities that contribute to the economy of the North of Scotland.

 Hunting, shooting and (nuclear) fission, plus that new one, revenueable energy.

Q What is a turbine?

A Something like a bandage an Arab or Shreik wears on his head. Maybe he is from Achinghead Road.

A student reliably informed his tutor that the four Ps of marketing were: *product*, *price*, *place*, *distribution*.

Describe what you know about the
Magdeburg Hemispheres.

 **Magdeburg was a German scientist with
balls seven feet in diameter and when he
attached two teams of horses to them, he
couldn't pull them apart.**

[Underneath the teacher has written: 'Oyah!']

 How do you change centimetres into
metres?

 Take out 'centi'.

How would you extract more energy from solar panels?

 Increase the power of the sun.

 What have you learned in geometry this term?

 I have learned to bisex angles.

Why, aerodynamically, would a racing motorcyclist lie over the petrol tank?

 To keep the petrol warm.

 Define parallel lines.

A Parallel lines never meet, unless you bend one or both of them.

If you had three apples and four oranges in one hand and four apples and three oranges in the other hand, what would you have?

 Pure huge hands.

 Explain an instance when you would use algebra.

Algebraical symbols are used when you do not know what you are talking about.

You arrive at a bus stop at 5 to 3 and the bus comes at 3.20. How long have you been waiting?

 Ages!

 Define a circle.

A **A circle is a line which meets its other end without ending.**

If it took eight men ten hours to build a wall, how long would it take four men to build it?

 Nae point. The wall is there already from the first guys.

 Explain total and remainder.

 The total is when you add up all the numbers and the remainder is what pulls Santa on his slay.

Q Name a component in a circuit.

A An anticipator.

Q What are cumulative frequency graphs?

A Cumulative frequency graphs are excellent ways of comparing the data. I used them to compare whether sex had an affect on how much television a person watched.

F'UN GREAT ONES

(b) The table shows some genotypes and phenotypes.

Genotype	Phenotype
A–B–	all fur black
aaB–	all fur white (albino)
a^{b}abb	white body fur with brown face, ears, legs and tail (Himalayan)

(i) What do the dashes represent in the genotype of the black rabbit?

Morse Code?

(1 mark)

Roll no - 420

Q1 Explain digestive system ?

ans Its a process that start with right hand & ends
with left .

Q2 What is the chemical formula for water ?

ans h,i,j,k,l,m,n,o   (h to o).

Q3 Till when second world war was fought ?

ans from page no 26 to page no 43 .

Q4 Who was Bhagat Singh ?

ans Ajay Davegan, Boby Deol, Manoj Kumar ,etc

Q5 Who was Adlof Hitler ?

ans this person.

$\frac{0}{10}$

A turtle makes progress when it sticks its neck out

This quote means that if you help out instead of keeping to yourself, you can make some progress. For example if you help out with the environment, it will make some progress, or some shit like that

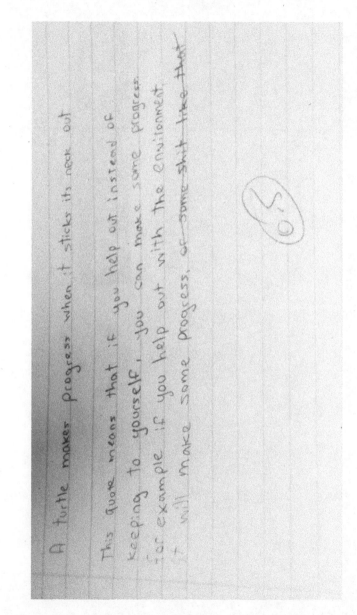

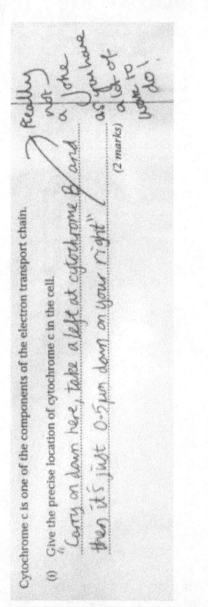

Cytochrome c is one of the components of the electron transport chain.

(i) Give the precise location of cytochrome c in the cell.

"Carry on down here, take a left at cytochrome B and then it's just 0.5 μm down on your right"

Really not a "you have as a lot of work to do!"

(2 marks)

(ii) Identify the **two** locations that hold most of the Earth's water.

North pole, South pole (Antarctica) where santa lives

[2]

F'un Great Ones

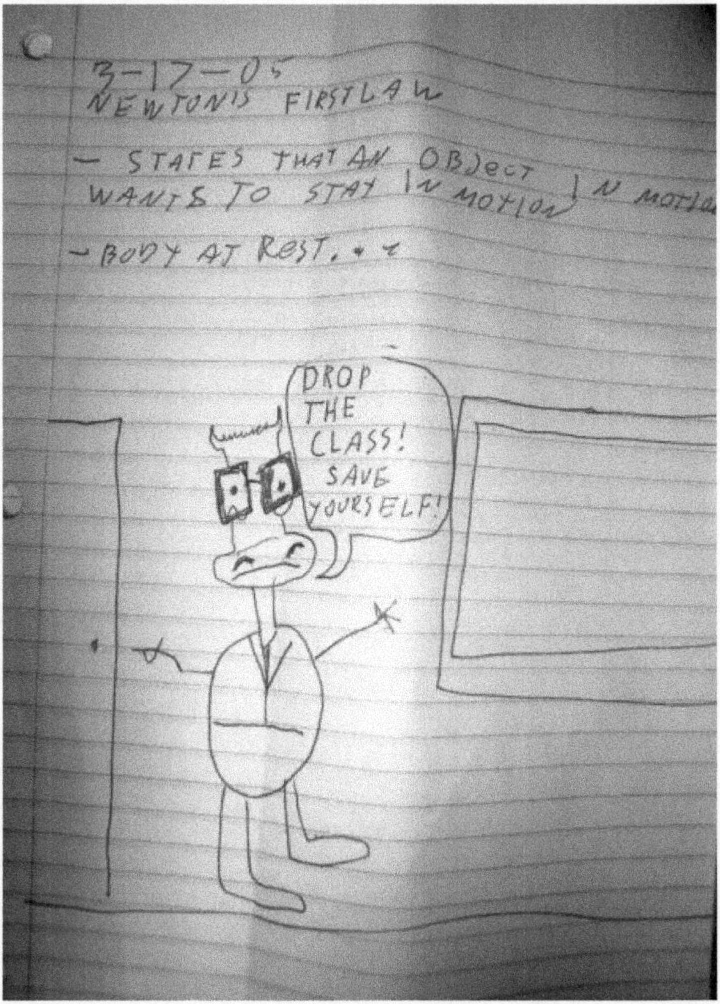

F'un Great Ones

The F7 key. Learn it. Use it. Love it.

Lasers in Everyday Life

Seems you can't go a single sentence without a typo.

It seems tat I cannot go a single day in a classroom without at least one of my professors using a laser pointer to enhance their lecture. This has been very beneficial to me, especially on the days that I forget to wear my glasses. Laser pointers are one of the more obvious and easily noticed lasers that effect our daily lives. One laser that is not so noticeable that I use daily is the laser that magically creates music from those shiny discs that I put into my CD player. My CD/DVD player gets used daily and without those tiny lasers that read and interpret data, I would be stuck with lousy cassette tapes again. As I mentioned before, I wear glasses and I often forget to wear tem. Someday, when I have a little money in the bank account, I plan to have laser surgery performed to correct my eyesight. Lasers have revolutionized the medical field with their precise ability to perform surgery that is safer, easier to perform and enables faster healing time for patients. One of the brightest lasers that I have ever seen belonged to an Astronomer. This Astronomer had a laser that could shine for 1.25 miles. This feature enabled him to teach a group of campers about the stars in the sky by actually pointing at exact stars without us having to guess where he was looking. Lasers are truly everywhere in our lives. They speed up checkouts at the supermarket, play music in your CD player, and help you change the television channel from the comfort of you couch.

This is a science course. Lasers are not voodoo, CD players are not magical.

Oh, someday... sight

True, True.

Yes, lasers make our lazy, excessive consumer lifestyle possible.

Really, you don't need to capitalize "astronomer" unless he's some sort of super hero.

NO! My telescope powers are useless against his LASER!

Next time... Will Astronomy Man SURVIVE?!

F'un Great Ones

(d) When acidified potassium permanganate is added to a solution of sodium iodide, a reaction occurs.

(i) Write a balanced equation for the reaction by writing balanced half equations and combining them.

MnO_4^- ⟶   Something

Something else   ⟶   Another thing

Stuff ⟶ other stuff

(ii) Which species is the oxidant (oxidising agent) in this reaction? 1st one ☒☒☒

Justify your answer   guess ☒☒☒

(iii) Describe what you would **observe** as this reaction took place. Link your **observations** to the **species** involved.

Add contents of packet and return to boil whilst stirring continuously. Simmer on a medium heat for 10 minutes.

- sauce will thicken on standing.

     Serves 4 ☒☒☒

Some people don't look up until they are flat on their backs.

This quote means some people can't look up because something has happened to their necks so they can't look up. For example, if a person gets kicked in the neck by a kung fu midget, they will not be able to look up.

SCIENCES

Give a solution to the problem of global warming with regard to methane.

 Cows produce large amounts of methane, so the problem could be solved by fitting them with Catholic converters. But the Proddies might object.

 Explain a method used to improve the quality of water in Loch Katrine.

 Flirtation is a good method. It takes out big polluting things like sand, grit, sheep crap and deid canoeists.

How is dew formed?

 The sun shines down on the leaves and they get a' sweaty.

 Describe a permanent set of teeth.

A permanent set of teeth consists of eight canines, eight cuspids, two molars, and eight cuspidors.

What causes the tides in the oceans?

 The tides are a fight between the earth and the moon. The moon is a planet just like the earth, only a lot deader. All water tends to flow towards the moon, because there is nae water on the moon, and nature abhors a flask, or something. I forget where the sun joins the fight.

Explain the composition of water.

 Water is composed of two gins, Oxygin and Hydrogin. Oxygin is pure gin. Hydrogin is water and gin.

Q Explain the growth and development of a city you have studied.

A *There are a lot of whorehouses in Glasgow's South side area.*

[Warehouses?]

Q Define a super saturated solution.

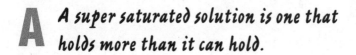

A *A super saturated solution is one that holds more than it can hold.*

The river Missouri flows in which state?

 Mainly liquid except maybe in winter. I've never been there.

 Give a reason why people would want to live near power lines.

 You get your electricity faster.

Q What is the Equator?

A The equator is a menagerie lion running round the earth through Africa.

Q Explain the meaning of the word 'germinate'.

A To become a naturalized German.

Name three typical Scottish dishes.

 A cup, a plate, and a wee saucer with a chip out of it.

 How does blood circulate?

A Blood flows down one leg and up the other.

Q Explain one of the consequences of the increase in electronic mail.

A Postman Pat will get the sack (joke) and then he would have to come off the telly. He would then be called Pat.

Q Name three kinds of blood vessels.

A Three kinds of blood vessels are arteries, vanes and caterpillars.

Explain ASCII.

 American Standard Code for Information Intercourse.

 How would you treat a dog bite?

A Put the dog away for several days. If it has not recovered, then kill it.

Describe how improvements in finance have been created by Information Technology.

 I.T. has helped to create 24-Hour Internet Bonking.

Q Where is the alimentary canal?

A The alimentary canal is located in the northern part of Scotland, near Inverness.

Q What are steroids?

A *Thae wee brass rod things for keeping carpets from moving on the stairs.*

 Q Describe the bonding in SO_2 in terms of orbital overlap and delocalised electrons.

A *It's pretty awesome.*

[Author's comment: Who would dispute that?]

Where is the semi circular canal?

 The semi circular canal is located in Indiana, which is either in America or near Pakistan.

 Name a type of fossil.

A *Margaret Thatcher, my dad says.*

Q What is the purpose of a skeleton?

A The skeleton is what is left after the insides have been taken out and the outsides have been taken off. The purpose of the skeleton is something to hang meat on.

 Q What is a dodo?

A The dodo is a bird that is almost decent by now.

Cotton buds carry a warning not to insert them into which part of the body?

 That is private. And I've tolt the doctor I won't do that any more.

 How does the hookworm larva enter the body?

 The hookworm larva enters the human body through the soul.

Name a major disease associated with
cigarettes.

 Premature death.

 How long does it take for the Earth to
go round the sun?

The Earth makes one resolution
every 24 hours.

Q What is an octopus?

A An octopus is an animal that has eight testicles.

Q How does the cuckoo raise chicks?

A The cuckoo bird does not lay his own eggs.

What would be your first check regarding a blood transfusion?

 Before giving a blood transfusion find out if the blood is affirmative or negative.

 How would you remove air from a flask?

 To remove air from a flask, fill it with water, tip the water out, and put the cork in dead quick before the air can get back in.

How do you deal with a foreign body in the eye?

 To remove dust from the eye, pull the eye down over the nose.

 What is the definition of a protein?

A protein is something that is made up of mean old acids.

Q How do you deal with drowning?

 A *Climb on top of the person and move up and down to make Artificial Perspiration.*

 Q What kind of tails do opossums have?

A **Reprehensible ones.**

Q How do you deal with fainting?

A Rub the person's chest or, if a lady, rub her arm above the hand instead. Or put the head between the knees of the nearest doctor.

Q What is the spinal column?

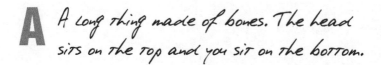 **A** A long thing made of bones. The head sits on the top and you sit on the bottom.

Q What is respiration?

 A *Respiration is composed of inspiration and then expectoration.*

 Q Name six animals that specifically live in the Arctic.

A *Two polar bears and four seals.*

Q Name a socially transmittable disease.

A Gentle herrpiece.

Q What do we call the science of classifying living things?

A Racism.

What is the collective name for the bones in the feet?

 My teacher said 'metal arseholes', but I don't think that's right.

 Why does ice float in water but sink in alcohol?

 If there was alcohol why would you waste good ice in water?

Q What is a seizure?

A *He was a Roman emperor. I think his first name was Augustus.*

Q DNA testing is important in?

A CSI Miami.

Q Discuss something that happens to your body as you age.

A *When you get old, so do your bowles, and you get intercontinental.*

Q Which gland secretes tears?

A The female gland.

Q What is artificial insemination?

A When the fermer does it to the bull instead of the coo.

[HND exam question in a Timber Technology paper.]

Q What is Dieldrin, what is it used for and why do environmentalists object to its use?

A It is used to kill woodworm and environmentalists object to its use because of the suffering and death it causes the woodworm.

Give the meaning of the term 'Caesarean section'.

 The Caesarean section is a district in Rome.

 Discuss the force of gravity.

 Gravity was invented by Issaac Walton. It is chiefly noticeable in the autumn when the apples are falling off the trees.

Q How can you delay milk turning sour?

A *Keep it in the coo.*

[A question about the Data Protection Act.]

 Q Give one example of an illegal use someone could make of the data.

A *You could use it to track someone down and devour their soul!*

How are the main parts of the body categorised? (e.g. The abdomen)

 The body is consisted into 3 parts – the brainium, the borax and the abdomen cavity. The brainium contains the brain, the borax contains the heart and lungs and the abdomen cavity contains the five bowels: A, E, I, O and U.

 Give an example of movement in plants, and an animal that cannot move.

 Tryphids and a dead cat.

Q What is a terminal illness?

A *It is when your Ma and Da take you on holiday and you get sick with excitement at the airport.*

Q What is selective breeding?

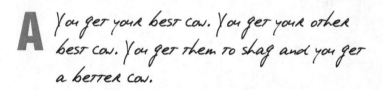

A You get your best cow. You get your other best cow. You get them to shag and you get a better cow.

How does a flower defend itself against predation by insects?

 The pistol of a flower is its only protection against insects.

Q Is a brick a solid, liquid or gas?

A *Yes.*

What do you count on a tree to tell its age?

 The coconuts.

 Give a description of a transformer.

It's a robot but is disguised as something else, like a car.

Which is rhubarb, fruit or vegetable?

 Rhubarb is a kind of celery went bloodshot. It is also a noise that actors make when they are working.

 Why do we cool down after exercise?

 To prevent the build up of galactic acid.

Name an individual non-competitive activity.

 Yoda.

[Small *Star Wars* character with pointy ears]

 Explain what you know about the ancient Olympics.

 In the old Olympic Games, Greek folk ran races, jumped, hurled the biscuits, and threw the javel in. I don't know what they threw the javel into.

Explain the concept of spin in party politics.

A spin is what my great granny at her afternoon tea parties used to put sugar in her tea with before she went to heaven. A spoon is what my Mum uses. It looks the same but it is bigger. The word is bigger I mean.

In a democratic society, how important are elections?

A

I don't understand that about democractic, but elections are very important. Sex can only happen when a male gets an election.

What is a planet?

 A planet is a body of earth surrounded by sky. Sometimes blue, but in Scotland more often it's no.

 What is a vacuum?

A large, empty space where the Pope lives in shameful luxury, our minister says.

What is the main reason for divorce?

 Getting married to a bitch, my Da says.

 Explain clearly, in your own words, what you think the term, 'privatisation of prisons' means.

A It means that prisoners will have the chance to buy their own cells.

Q What would be the course of action if your tv screen showed the message, 'The following programme contains flashing images'?

A 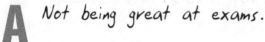 Move your seat closer. There might be naked folk.

Q What is the main reason for failure?

A Not being great at exams.

F'un Exams

 Name a bird with a long neck.

 Naomi Campbell. And that other wan, the Scottish wan.

 What would be your treatment for a head cold?

 For a head cold: use an agonizer to spray the nose until it drops in your throat.

Q Describe an experiment with sulphur.

A To collect fumes of sulphur, hold a deacon over a flame in a test tube.

Q Where can nitrogen be found?

A *Nitrogen is not found in Ireland, because it is not found in a free state.*

Describe the qualities of a magnet.

 Something you can find crawling over a dead cat.

 Describe two states of water.

A H_2O is hot water. CO_2 is cold water.